GREAT OUTDOORS
SPORTS ZONE

SALTWATER
FISHING
SNAPPER, MACKEREL, BLUEFISH, TUNA, AND MORE

Tom Carpenter

Lerner Publications Company • Minneapolis

Lerner Publications Company
A division of Lerner Publishing Group, Inc.
241 First Avenue North
Minneapolis, MN 55401 U.S.A.
Website address: www.lernerbooks.com

Content Consultant: James G. Dickson, PhD, wildlife biologist, researcher, author, professor, hunter, and angler

Library of Congress Cataloging-in-Publication Data

Carpenter, Tom, 1962-
    Saltwater fishing : snapper, mackerel, bluefish, tuna, and more / by Tom Carpenter.
        p.   cm. — (Great outdoors sports zone)
    Includes index.
    ISBN 978-1-4677-0220-1 (lib. bdg. : alk. paper)
        1. Saltwater fishing—Juvenile literature. 2. Marine fishes—Juvenile literature. I. Title.
SH457.C317 2013
    799.16—dc23   2012007053

Manufactured in the United States of America
1 – CG – 7/15/12

The images in this book are used with the permission of: Backgrounds: © Vtls/Shutterstock Images; © Sabri Deniz Kizil/Shutterstock Images; © Alexander A. Sobolev/Shutterstock Images; © Slobodan Djajic/Shutterstock Images; © mountainpix/Shutterstock Images, p. 5; © Library of Congress, pp. 6 (LC-USZ62-136570), 7 (LC-USZ62-13912), p. 9 (LC-USE6-D-008935); © North Wind/North Wind Picture Archives, p. 8; © Jim Lopes/Shutterstock Images, p. 10; © Stephan Kerkhofs/Shutterstock Images, p. 11 (top); © J.D.S./Shutterstock Images, p. 11 (bottom); © Steve Hillebrand/USFWS, pp. 12, 13; © fimkaJane/Shutterstock Images, p. 14; © Yuri Arcurs/Shutterstock Images, p. 15 (top); © Red Line Editorial, pp. 15 (bottom), 24 (top), 28; © Vtls/Shutterstock Images, p. 16; © ARENA Creative/Shutterstock Images, p. 17 (top); © Marcin Balcerzak/Shutterstock Images, p. 17 (bottom); © bikeriderlondon/Shutterstock Images, p. 18; © David Meardon/USFWS, p. 19; © Sherrianne Talon/Shutterstock Images, p. 20; © littleny/Shutterstock Images, p. 21; © Shinga/Shutterstock Images, p. 22; © luxxtek/iStockphoto, p. 23 (top); © Sielemann/Shutterstock Images, p. 23 (bottom); © Norman Bateman/Shutterstock Images, p. 24 (bottom); © holbox/Shutterstock Images, pp. 25, 26 (bottom), 27 (bottom right); © Jorge Gonzalez/iStockphoto, p. 26 (top); © Richard Gunion/iStockphoto, p. 26 (middle); © HelleM/Shutterstock Images, p. 27 (top); © Jiang Hongyan/Shutterstock Images, p. 27 (top middle); © Keith Publicover/Shutterstock Images, p. 27 (bottom left); © Elena Gaak/Shutterstock Images, p. 29.
Front Cover: © Claus Christensen/Photographer's Choice/Getty Images.

Main body text set in Avenir LT Std 65 Medium 11/17.
Typeface provided by Adobe Systems.

TABLE OF CONTENTS

CHAPTER ONE

WHY GO SALTWATER FISHING?

There's something special about fishing in the salty ocean. You get to spend time outside enjoying fresh air and stunning views. You never know what you will catch. You might land a snapper or a flounder—or you might even hook a shark! Fresh seafood is good for you and tastes great.

Saltwater fishing is easy and fun. You don't need to be rich or own a huge boat to do it. Fishers, also called anglers, can catch all kinds of fish without ever leaving land. Fishing from a boat is fun too. You might know someone who has a boat. You can also go out on a boat for hire, called a charter boat.

Commercial fishing crews make their livings on the ocean. Sport fishers fish for pleasure. These different kinds of fishing can exist together because commercial crews often target different species (kinds of fish) and fishing areas than sport anglers do.

No matter what kind of fishing you are doing, ocean fish are hungry and willing to bite. Plus, they put up an exciting fight! So pick up your rod and reel, grab that bucket of bait, and let's get going.

It's hard to beat the excitement of saltwater fishing.

CHAPTER TWO
HISTORY OF SALTWATER FISHING

Native Americans were the first anglers in North America. For them, fishing was a way of gathering food. They used many different fishing techniques.

They wove reed traps called weirs. They hung these structures between poles and placed them in shallow water where fish tended to travel. Native American anglers would scoop out the trapped fish. They also used nets made from animal hair to fish from a beach or deeper water.

A Native American man of the Yurok people of California uses a net to try to catch fish from the beach.

Kayaks (small canoes) helped Native Americans, such as this man in Alaska, get closer to saltwater fish.

Spearing fish was another common technique. Sometimes, anglers would walk quietly in shallow water and thrust spears into fish. Other times, Native Americans would use a gig (a short spear with pointy hooks at the end). Sometimes they tied a rope to the gig so they could throw it and then pull back the fish. They used kayaks or other boats to fish in deeper water.

Native Americans also used hooks and fishing line. They carved hooks from wood or bone. Then they tied these hooks to lines woven from plant fibers.

Settlers Arrive

European settlers started to arrive in North America in the 1500s. They brought commercial fishing techniques from their homelands. The settlers used big boats powered by sails and the wind. These boats could also be rowed when the wind was calm. They used a gill net to catch many fish at one time. Fish would swim into the net and get caught by their gills (slits for breathing).

In the mid-1800s, saltwater anglers used boats and nets to catch fish off the Atlantic coast.

By the early 1900s, commercial fishers were taking in huge hauls of fish. This put some fish populations in danger.

Ocean fish were plentiful when settlers arrived. But techniques improved as more settlers started fishing. More and more fish were taken out of the ocean. Modern sport fishing in North America developed in the early 1900s. People had more time and money to fish for fun. Many people lived and fished along the coasts of the Atlantic Ocean, the Pacific Ocean, and the Gulf of Mexico. Soon, sport and commercial fishing hurt the populations of many fish species. Some were even in danger of becoming extinct (completely killed off). Then the idea of conservation (the smart use of natural resources) took hold.

CHAPTER THREE

FISH FOR THE FUTURE

Managing fish populations in the ocean is a big challenge. More than 70 percent of our planet is covered by salt water. Plus, different countries fish the same ocean. That means there must be international standards and rules for commercial and sport fishing.

The ocean has many fish. Some fish live close to shore where you can catch them. Others live far offshore in very deep water. Different fish have different habitat needs. A habitat is the area in which a fish lives, spawns (lays eggs), finds food, and hides for safety.

Different fish live in different parts of the ocean. Some live close enough to shore that you can catch them from a rocky beach.

The ocean may seem full of fish, but fishing regulations are important for keeping fish populations healthy.

Providing good habitats with clean water is the best way to support healthy fish populations. The ocean may be huge, but it is delicate. Thoughtless behavior by individuals and fishing crews can endanger the ocean. We all share the job of taking care of this resource.

NO DUMPING DRAINS TO OCEAN

The first step in protecting saltwater fish populations is protecting their habitat.

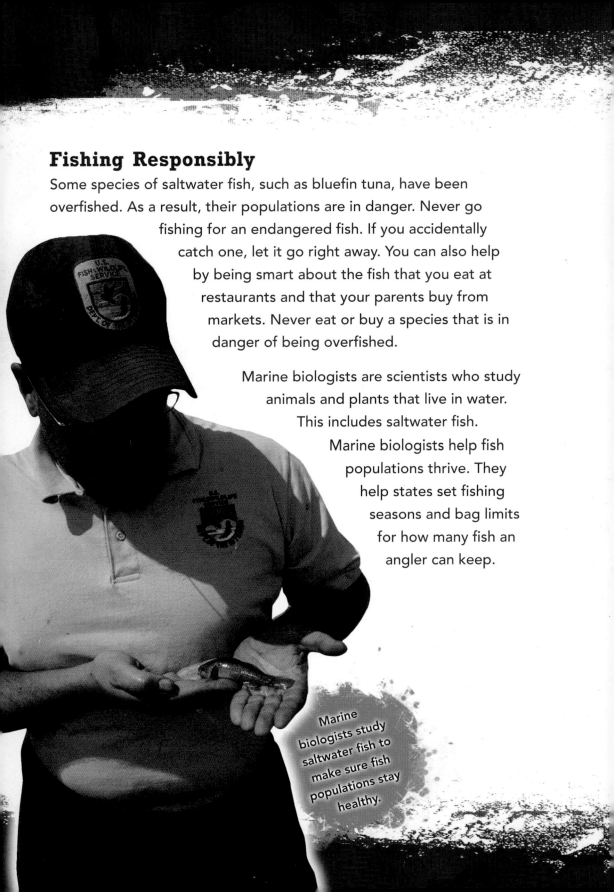

Fishing Responsibly

Some species of saltwater fish, such as bluefin tuna, have been overfished. As a result, their populations are in danger. Never go fishing for an endangered fish. If you accidentally catch one, let it go right away. You can also help by being smart about the fish that you eat at restaurants and that your parents buy from markets. Never eat or buy a species that is in danger of being overfished.

Marine biologists are scientists who study animals and plants that live in water. This includes saltwater fish. Marine biologists help fish populations thrive. They help states set fishing seasons and bag limits for how many fish an angler can keep.

Marine biologists study saltwater fish to make sure fish populations stay healthy.

You can be fined for fishing without a license. Make sure you buy a fishing license and follow all other regulations.

Fishing seasons ensure that fishing takes place when the fish aren't spawning or protecting their young. Bag limits let you keep only a reasonable number of fish so the population isn't hurt. An ocean may seem endless, but it isn't. Fish populations are not endless either. All saltwater anglers must purchase a fishing license or permit. Fishing licenses provide important money to help manage fish and their habitats.

Do your part to help protect ocean fish. Follow all fishing rules, regulations, and bag limits. Fish only for species with healthy populations. Protect fish habitats by working to cut down on ocean pollution.

CHAPTER FOUR

GEARING UP AND GETTING READY

It's time to get ready for saltwater fishing. You need to choose the right gear. You also need to know how to land (bring in) a fish and how to fish safely.

Rod and Reel

Rods and reels hold your line and help you cast your bait. Baitcasting or spinning reels are the best for saltwater fishing. Baitcasting reels are sturdy and cast a long way. You need to keep your thumb on the spool to stop the line from tangling. Spinning reels are open-faced and hang below the rod. They are easier to cast than baitcasting reels but are not quite as sturdy.

Rods are important for casting and for fighting fish. Graphite is a good rod material because it is sensitive for feeling bites. But it is also tough and flexible enough for fighting fish.

Baitcasting reel

Fishing Line

Fishing line is your only direct tie to the fish you just hooked and are reeling in. Monofilament line is good for saltwater fishing. Monofilament line is made of a single strand of a man-made material, such as nylon. Different types of lines have different strengths. Stronger lines are better for bigger fish.

Hooks and Sinkers

A sinker is a weight on your line that helps hold your line down in the water. It takes your bait down to where the fish are. A hook holds the bait, and then catches the fish's mouth when the fish bites the bait. Hooks come in different shapes and sizes. The bigger the fish you are going after, the bigger the hook you need.

TYING A PALOMAR KNOT

1. Fold fishing line, and thread loop of line through eye of hook.

2. Pull line over and under itself, leaving a small loop.

3. Pull loop around hook.

4. Pull tight.

Chum is ground-up fish or fish guts that are used as bait. Put the chum into a net bag in the water. The chum will attract small baitfish (small fish eaten by larger fish). Game fish will follow. You can buy chum or make your own out of what's left after you clean your catch. You can freeze chum in a bag for your next fishing trip.

Fishing Bait

Some saltwater anglers use natural bait. Natural bait might be frozen, live animals such as worms and minnows. It can also be fresh meat, called cut bait. Natural bait takes some work to get and prepare, but it is worth it. Fish can't resist the real thing.

Many artificial lures are designed to look like the smaller fish big fish like to eat.

Other anglers prefer to use artificial lures. These are bait made from plastic, wood, or other materials to look like real fish food. Some of the best plastic artificial lures look like baitfish. Jigs are another effective lure. They are often tipped with soft plastic tails, feathers, or natural bait.

Other Gear

Thin wire leaders attach your hook or lure to the line. The wires keep a sharp-toothed fish from biting through your line and getting away. A landing net helps you bring in a big fish. A long-handled hook called a gaff works well to land fish you don't plan on releasing (letting go of).

A tackle box keeps all your fishing gear organized.

A tackle box or bag holds your gear. Pliers and a knife help you change your hook and lure combination. A cooler with ice holds the fish you plan to keep and eat.

Fishing Safety

Safety is important when fishing on the ocean. Always wear a life jacket, even if you know how to swim. A life jacket keeps your head above water even if you hit your head on a rock or you faint from the cold water. Ocean waves can be very strong. Never wade in the ocean to fish unless you are with an adult.

Watch the weather. If a storm is coming, stop fishing and get to a safe place. Catching a few more fish isn't worth risking your life with lightning or rough seas.

Consider the safety of others when you are fishing. Always look behind you before casting. You don't want to hook a friend or a parent.

Even if you are a strong swimmer, it's a good idea to wear a life jacket when you are near the ocean.

CHAPTER FIVE

GOING FISHING

Now that you're geared up, it's time to go fishing. But first you need to know when and where to go. While saltwater fishing is always fun, certain times and conditions are best. You also need to know how to set the hook, play (reel in) fish, and care for your catch.

Catching a fish can be very exciting. But spending time near the ocean can be fun even if you go home empty-handed.

Morning and evening are great times to fish because this is when fish are out looking for food.

Best Fishing Conditions

Fishing can be good any time of day or night. Fish come into shallower water to feed when the light is low, so morning and evening are great times to fish. Fishing is often good on days when the weather is changing and clouds are rolling in.

Tide

The moon's gravitational pull causes low and high tides, which are up-and-down movements of the ocean's water level. Fishing is best during the first hour or so when the tide changes and water levels begin to rise or drop. The sea level can be very different at low and high tide. Pay attention to the high tide and low tide times so you don't get stuck at your fishing spot.

BLUE-WATER FISHING

Blue-water fishing is also called offshore fishing. This type of fishing is done in very large boats. They travel far offshore, trolling (slowly dragging bait) for big game fish, such as swordfish, sailfish, big tuna, and marlin. These fish are sometimes more than 100 miles (160 kilometers) offshore. Anglers use sturdy rods and big reels to battle these fish. Some fish might weigh more than 400 pounds (181 kilograms). Maybe someday you'll get the chance to go on a blue-water adventure.

Bottom Fishing

Bottom fishing is the kind of fishing anglers often do from piers (long docks), jetties (structures that extend into the ocean), in the surf, and sometimes from a boat. A weight takes your bait underwater to the sea bottom. When the tip of the rod starts moving or you feel tugs, you've got a fish!

Pier Fishing

Piers are easy to find along the oceanfront. Many piers are open to the public for fishing. Others are private and charge a small fee. Most piers are very long and stretch far from shore. They give you access to deeper water. Make sure fishing is allowed or you have permission to fish from a pier.

You can catch a lot of great fish from a pier without ever getting on a boat.

Jetty Fishing

A jetty provides feeding and hiding places for baitfish, which in turn attract bigger fish. Be careful on wet jetty rocks. Wear shoes that will grip the rocks. Cast your bait away from the jetty so you don't snag your line on the rocks. When bringing in a fish, keep it above the rocks.

Jetties are designed to protect shoreline or harbors from waves. They also make great fishing spots.

Surf Fishing

Anglers who surf fish cast their lines from sandy or gravelly beaches. Sometimes they will even wade into the water. Baitfish like the shallow water near the surf. Look for gulls and other waterbirds diving in the water. That tells you a school of baitfish is nearby, and this means the game fish are close behind. You can bottom fish in the surf or cast artificial lures. Be careful of ocean currents and tides when wading.

When surf fishing, you cast your line directly from a beach.

When artificial bait is trolled behind a boat, it looks real to hungry fish.

Trolling

If you have a boat, trolling is a great way to fish because you cover a lot of water. To troll, move very slowly in a boat, pulling bait behind you. Most anglers troll with artificial baits.

Drifting

Drifting is another kind of fishing you can do from a boat. Drift along likely fish spots with your bait dragging behind you in the water. Anglers typically use natural bait when drifting.

Fly-Fishing

Some saltwater fishing is done with fly-fishing gear. A rod, reel, and line work together to cast the line that floats with a leader and a fly (a lure made of feathers that floats or sinks). These flies are tied to look like baitfish, insects, crabs, or other fish food. A lot of saltwater fly-fishing is done in shallow water. Anglers wade in the water, casting as they walk.

Fly lure

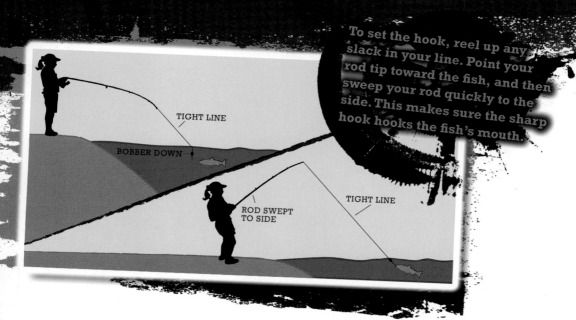

To set the hook, reel up any slack in your line. Point your rod tip toward the fish, and then sweep your rod quickly to the side. This makes sure the sharp hook hooks the fish's mouth.

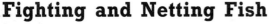

Setting the Hook

When you get a bite, you must set the hook. This means to firmly get the hook caught in the fish's mouth. Don't just start reeling, or you'll pull the bait out of the fish's mouth.

Fighting and Netting Fish

Fighting fish is fun. They tug, circle, pull, thrash, and jump! Keep the tip of the rod fairly high and keep reeling. Don't let your line go slack, or the hook will fall out.

Getting your fish in the boat can be one of the toughest parts of saltwater fishing.

Here's how to release a fish so it can live to fight again:

- Play the fish quickly so it doesn't get overtired.
- Wet your hands before handling a fish. Dry hands remove a fish's protective slime coating.
- Check for any teeth or fins on the fish that could hurt you.
- Remove the hook quickly.
- If the hook is deep, just cut your line. The fish's digestive juices will dissolve the hook.
- Slide or slip the fish gently into the water. Do not toss it.
- To help a tired fish, hold it in the water by its tail and gently move it forward and backward.
- Watch it swim away!

A net will help you bring your catch safely into the boat.

To net a fish with a landing net, always lead the fish into the net headfirst. It helps to have someone else do the netting. You can also use a gaff to get your fish in the boat. You can grab a fish by the lips to land it. Before you touch a fish, look for sharp teeth or fins that could hurt you. Don't touch a fish's delicate gills.

Caring for Your Catch

If you want to save some fish to eat, keep them fresh. Put fish that you want to keep on ice in a cooler. Do not leave fish dead and floating in a bucket or on a stringer (wire or string) that some anglers use to hold the fish they've caught.

SALTWATER GAME FISH GUIDE

RED SNAPPER

Snappers live almost everywhere. The red snapper is most common along the Atlantic coast and in the Gulf of Mexico. A red snapper can weigh 20 pounds (9 kg) or more. You can catch snappers in rocky areas. Good red snapper baits include squid, clams, or worms.

SUMMER FLOUNDER

Flounders flip sand over themselves to hide and then wait for a meal (usually fish) to swim past. Both of a flounder's eyes are on one side of its head. A 15-pound (6.8-kg) summer flounder is a great catch. Live minnows or other baitfish and live shrimp make good bait. Use any kind of bottom fishing rig. Artificial lures also work well.

BLUEFISH

Bluefish are very popular along the Atlantic coast. You can catch bluefish from shore, often near rocks, where they feed on baitfish and crabs. They usually weigh up to 15 pounds (6.8 kg). Bluefish have very sharp teeth, so use a wire leader. Live bait works best. But flashy, artificial lures will work too.

SEA TROUT

You can catch sea trout in shallow water, such as mud flats and saltwater marshes. A 5-pound (2.2-kg) sea trout is an excellent catch. Live baitfish and shrimp make good bait.

SPANISH MACKEREL

Mackerel are members of the tuna family. An average Spanish mackerel weighs 2 to 3 pounds (0.9 to 1.3 kg). Mackerel feed in shallow water or near the water's surface. This makes them good targets for jetty, pier, or surf anglers. Mackerel gather in big schools that chase baitfish. Chum attracts baitfish, which then bring in mackerel. Both live and artificial bait work well.

COHO SALMON

You can catch several different species of salmon along the Pacific coast. Salmon are hatched in freshwater. Then they swim to the ocean where they spend most of their lives. They return to the stream where they were born to spawn. An average coho salmon weighs 8 pounds (3.6 kg). Trolling is a great way to catch salmon. Use a colorful, artificial lure.

TUNA

To catch a tuna, you'll have to fish from a boat many miles offshore. Tuna are strong fighters. When you hook one, hold on! Different tuna species include albacore, blackfin, skipjack, and yellowfin. The biggest tuna is the bluefin, which can grow to weigh as much as 1,400 pounds (635 kg). Some species of tuna are in danger of being overfished, so know which species are OK to catch. The best natural bait is live or fresh fish.

HOW TO PREPARE YOUR FISH

Filleting your catch means removing the skin and cutting off the fish's meat. This gets rid of most of the bones. You can also scale a fish and remove its head and guts. Then pick out the bones after you cook it. Ask for an adult's help with filleting, scaling, and cooking your fish.

How to Clean and Fillet a Fish

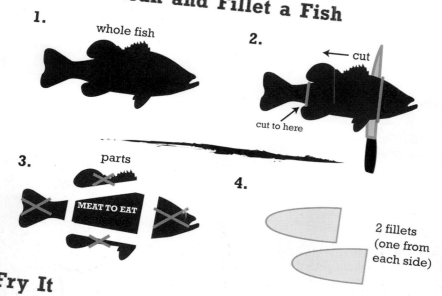

1. whole fish

2. cut / cut to here

3. parts / MEAT TO EAT / scales off

4. 2 fillets (one from each side)

Fry It

Heat a half inch (1 centimeter) of vegetable oil in a skillet. Roll the fish pieces in flour or cornmeal seasoned with salt, pepper, and garlic powder. Fry the fish until the outsides are crispy and golden brown, about three to four minutes per side.

Grill It

Brush the fillets with melted butter and a little olive oil. Then grill them over medium heat for three to four minutes per side. Squeeze lemon juice over each side after two to three minutes.

Bake It

Brush the fillets with melted butter and a little oil. Place a fillet or two, two cut-up carrots, and one cut-up potato on a piece of aluminum foil. Sprinkle all ingredients with salt and pepper. Then wrap the foil into a package. Place in a 350°F (175°C) oven, on a grill on low heat, or in coals for an hour. A complete meal!

Taco-ize It

Cut up fish into small pieces, fry them, and use them as the meat in tacos with shredded lettuce, fresh salsa, guacamole, and shredded cheese.

After a long day out on the water, grilled salmon tastes delicious.

29

GLOSSARY

CONSERVATION

the thoughtful, efficient, and careful use of natural resources

GAME FISH

the kind of fish that sport anglers pursue most

JETTY

a long structure, often made of rocks, extending into the ocean

MONOFILAMENT

a kind of line often used for fishing made from a single strand of man-made fiber

NATURAL RESOURCES

things found in nature that are useful for humans

PIER

an elevated platform that extends into the ocean

SPECIES

animals that are grouped together by scientists because they are related

SURF

the rolling waves coming onto a beach

TIDE

the up-and-down movement of ocean water

TROLL

to fish by pulling live or artificial bait very slowly behind a boat

FOR MORE INFORMATION

Further Reading

Carpenter, Tom. *Freshwater Fishing: Bass, Trout, Walleye, Catfish, and More.* Minneapolis: Lerner Publications Company, 2013.

Hirschi, Ron. *Salmon.* Minneapolis: Lerner Publications Company, 2001.

Kamberg, Mary-Lane. *Saltwater Fishing.* New York: Rosen Central, 2012.

Websites

Fish Kids
http://www.epa.gov/waterscience/fish/kids/
This website from the Environmental Protection Agency has games and stories designed to teach kids about which fish are safe to eat.

Seafood Choices
http://www.pbs.org/emptyoceans/choices.html
This website includes links to sites that teach people how to make smart choices when buying saltwater fish to help keep fish populations healthy.

Take Me Fishing
http://www.takemefishing.org/fishing/saltwater-fishing/what-is-saltwater-fishing
This website features saltwater fishing tips, including where to go and what gear to bring.

INDEX

About the Author

Tom Carpenter has hunted and fished across North America for almost five decades, pursuing big game, waterfowl, upland birds, wild turkeys, small game, and fish of all kinds. He has raised three sons as sportsmen and written countless articles and contributed to dozens of books on hunting, fishing, nature, and the outdoors.